Fudge

Filled

Space

Poems by Bernard A. Goldberg

Also by Bernard A. Goldberg:

Necessary Illusions in Becoming a Jew
    in the Diaspora (1989)
    ISBN 0-9624348-0-9

Abel's Legacy and Other Hundredth
    Generation Survival Poems (1994)
    ISBN 0-9624348-1-7

Social Consequences of the Big Con
    in the Reading and Writing Game (1994)
    ISBN 0-9624348-2-5

For information, address Bernard A.
Goldberg, P.O. Box 255075, Sacramento,
California 95865.

ISBN 0-9624348-4-1

To the Coffee House
Poets,
Especially
To Ana and Phil,
Who Opened the Door

CONTENTS

Any artist knows
the difficulty of crafting
a straight line
and the ease of recording
a squiggle,
and even the straight
must be fudged
with illusion.

Fudged With Illusion

SPIN A RING AROUND THE POET

Spin a ring around the poet!
Keep your distance!
Never linger!
He's enchanted!
Do not let him
Touch your finger!

Spin a ring around the poet!
Block your ears!
Don't dare listen
As he counts
His measured chants!
Whoops! Too late!
He's caught your glance!

Spin a ring around the poet!
Kick the can
And see him chase!
Don't be caught!
He'll hold you captive!
Olly oxen! Hide your face!

Spin a ring around the poet!
Hurry on

Or he'll beguile!
Whoops! Too late!
He's caught your smile!

Spin a ring around the poet!
Glance and smile
Are his to keep!
You've paid the price:
Now take your profit,
A thought or two.
The cost is cheap!

NOT THE CAP THAT MARKS THE FOOL

Not the cap
That marks the fool
Nor the bells,
For any dunce
Can don the tools
And coin a verse to sing.

Not the plaid
That breaks the rule
And secrets tell,
For any clod
Can clown in school
And glibly gain a ring.

'Tis his wisdom
Marks him strange
And marks him well,
For only he
Can chance a change
And safely shock a king.

THE POETIC VALUE OF BETWEENS AND BEYONDS
WHILE VERSIFYING AT THE GUILD COFFEE HOUSE

The poem is not the verse,

But the spaces,

The interruptions,

The betweens

And beyonds,

The breaths,

The coughs,

The Shhh!

The scrape of a chair,

The whisper,

The knowing glance,

The smile,

The closed eyes,

The furled lip,

The exchanged note,

The bouncing ball,

The call for quiet,

The rattle of cupped ice.

No, the verse is not the poem,

But the linguistic catalyst

Without which

The intruding life

That contains it

Could never exist.

INSERT TO MATCH
STREET NOISE

Varoom! Varoom!
I intrude your room!
I am the poem!
Your time will come
soon!

OR

Urrase! Urrase!
I take your place!
I am the poem!
Withdraw your case!

INCENTIVE

Approval is a hell of a thing.
We'll commit crimes to get it.

The trouble is we bend and scrape
And try to please the ones who voice
Their negative traits
Because they think
That we'll approve
Because they have, in turn,
Misjudged our own intent
From what we said
As one attempt
To win their strong approval.

TENDER TOKEN
(LANDING ON THE MOON)

really, tender barman, certainty tells us
(although it told us, we admit, wrong before
no sane proprietor would veil
his brightest tempting light
leaving only token reality
for these lunatic faithful--
unistarstared, eyesore, groping in darkbar,
lying t' reason their way back to faith
as their lunar goddess
takes a final break and goes home。
vying with certain vehemence,
they seek the nowdimmed revelations
of earlier cutcrystal steinstars
and reflected faces--
in absence of lightsource, nowdimmed。

now how o tender barman could ya let em
louse up le lune?
or put it this way tender:
whatcha gonna do ta set it all straight?
nobody but nobody needs a drink
more than the poor old loonytic
only how's he find a bar even on nobhill
without the nutty lamp?
(notice how i talk in an informal bounce

18

off the shoulder when i've had a few)
o..k. tender has th message reacned ya
at st petes yet?
yer jus gonna hafta put fancy back in orbit
if ya spect th night to nourish th loonies
on yer enriched nectar
yer always groanin n moanin about.
or will i have trouble gettin hi enuf
to sink in?
(y cn spect a ver lil bit a incoherence
ever so often)

bfore ya cause a uproar count t seven
n cry bub
cz wen um grunk uv godall th yanswers
in mu finaleaning.
stop foolin with numbers n tears ya mot
n step outa this drag?
ok so tell ya wut: find yrself
a neat new loonar img kid.
get th ltr ritn school tchr type
huz an inside chic
and nobody cd hlp moonin ovr see
now then a crse shell hav ta fit
inta sm poetic dmnshuns
on that loonar srfc too--a crse
so once ya founder fixrup in a blanket

to kpr wrm n a miniskrt t kpr cl
an setr at th end uv yr bar
t lite the loonies lives
an wen th tv fakey livin clr
at the othr end a th bar
shows em pickin apart le lune
yal hav a jenuwine tru bonnie blue
liten up yr bar tender an puttin things
bk tgether
n fancyl be in orbit agen.

APPLE-TRIP TYCH IN EIGHT PARTS
(In which the philosophical questions and
the reader's indulgence are begged with
a minimum of humility.)
                    1
"This sitting can sure beat you up!"
    I heard her say.
    My tush couldn't agree more,
    pressed as it was on the oil-temperad
    guache deck
    dripdrop Pollacked splotches
    over hardwood concrete
    on the fifth floor of layers
    of the same set in the bedrock
    on a continental shelf in the corner
    of a Manahatta room.

But--and I say it with deliberate
    posterior pain--
    I had mistaken her words,
    my head as usual the Lewis Stein
    instrument of wild delusions
    of one of its anatomical extensions.

Something in my squirm and my instant
    reach to comfort my postal part
    prompted her luckily to repeat
    her comment, giving the whole
    incident a significance
    far above the floor
    on which we sat.

"This city has sure eaten him up!"
    she repeated kindly in my behalf,
    sensing that the second recital
    might for the first time
    penetrate my pigment.

With surprisingly little trouble,
    I transferred my posternal pain
    to my heart, nodding my head
                              21

in agreement,
shifting my pained look to a sad,
raising my sympathies above my belt.

She referred, of course, to our host,
    John Ford--the Irishbound Ford
    of explosive artistry,
    the deeply melancholy Ford
    whose loco frenzy motive has steamed
    its way finally to sunlight
    through the stubble-strewn
    tunnel of romantic darkness.

As soon as I nodded, though,
    I knew I was wrong.
    Before us stood not the eatee
    but the eater.
    In his solitary rebellion, he had
    assembled the street in its own image,
    fragmented, furnaced within,
    impersonal, threatening,
    and had given it form,
    digesting its height and weight
    to two dimensions and hanging them
    against the conventional
    flat-white of the world.

2

Clinging together in the darkness
    of a Brooklyn street,
    past the "Memory of Johnny C."
    abstract monument to a kid who
    thought he was concrete sprayed
    on manmade bricks of a falling wall,
    we spoke out loud against the dark,
    lest we--the Guardian Angels of the
    Art World--be abstracted ourselves.
    For given the choice, I'd rather be

a pisher than a portrait
that Johnny would never see.

Blindly tagging the fastest or tallest,
    lurching through the darkness
    after a canary coat past the old,
    neoned Daily Planet clock tower,
    we trusted Clark Kent's xray
    or Don Hazlitt's abstract vision
    to keep us out of trouble.

Out of the cold and into the warmth
    of Hazlitt's home
    and Josephine's coffee welcome,
    drawn by the crescents and circles
    and halves and quarters, we enter
    the partial-world of an artist's mind,
    abandoned to search the gesso
    for meaning.

A foot here, a face there, scattered
    over the universal canvas,
    the image gradually coalescing
    in the nervous Hazlitt laugh,
    as shy as it is assertive,
    and the unfunny Mr. Grin,
    wrenching with the angst
    of human longing,
    frozen forever in degrading
    payment for a lifetime
    of purrs and furs.

Down the tube and under the river
    the telegraffittisub
    communiports us westward
    to the eastside orient
    where we are consumed with a feast,
    where our fortunes confirm
    our history,
    and where I refuse to accept
    an empty cookie as my answer.
    Lucky in love, congenial and kind,

23

but G-d helps those who grab
a second cookie.

3

Focused in stopped light, the pastel
    pounders lie there, stripped
    of their use, begging for meaning.
    "I think I have it!"
    she claimed--perhaps exclaimed--
    pulling my sleeve toward
    the Lewis Steinhammers as she does
    occasionally on a day off at home
    in Spring whan a nail needs nailing.
    "The colors relate!" she rejoiced.
    "The pink handle and the pink head
    belong together, but they're not.
    And the purple box pants for the
    nextdoor purple head. There is
    order in chaos, after all!"
    she said.

I take some license in my report of the
    incident, but I could not agree
    with her principle more.
    She had discovered the key
    that could open the boxes
    and transport the pieces
    back from the desert of painted art
    again into the tules of utility.

What should the artist think!
    Giving meaning--or worse, use--
    to his pink!
    Rarity of rarities, who should walk by
    but the Lewis himself
    the Stein of all Steins,
    the mysterious, innocent bystander
    Stein, the one who records

the recorders betimes,
and sells them to thieves
as mementos of crimes.

The Stein of the cake cupped
so beauteous to see
the foolishly, droolishly cup
iced for tea,
luckily also the Stein
with the answers
to give her the faith to try
once again to unravel the yarn
told in art now and then。

She asked and he answered。
It was obvious at once
that he cared not a jot
her heart he might rend:
"I see you have found
what I didn't intend。"
The cad! Poor girl!
She was forced to recoup
before bolting the place
with the rest of the group。

4

From useless to use is distinction
quite faint。
In the world of the artist
no more than thin paint。
For us it was leaving the mad world
of Stein and entering
Golub's depiction of crime。

Hung on the crimson wall--perhaps hanged
is correct--the face of a Black
contorted with pain
surrounded by brothers
resigned to their duty,

defending their homeland
defined by the frame of their own rack,
setting the course of another,
future ship of state that will soon
ply the waters of the Cape
looking for deadly revenge
and gouging it
from its own body.

The Lion of Golub scrapes in his loft
seeking the nerve endings
in a lifeless body of canvas,
determined through some
heroic measure to return life
to a dead past.
Unable to find a concrete
grounding that will shift
with the inevitable distortion
of his ideal,
he punches reluctant holey grommets
and compromises reality
with movable nails.

5

From the illusion of reality
to the reality of illusion
we climb down from Golubian heights
understanding better
the violent street below
and elevate ourselves
to the fleshpots
of Pearlstinian magic.

Never has a five-by-seven wall
held so much flesh
and so little s-e-x.
One feels the necessity to spell,
thus disarming the s-word

and the conception it represents,
pushing it backward at best
to the confines of some garden
beyond memory
where apples were still apples,
navels were not navels
and knowledge? Who knows?

I know for a fact one thing for sure:
   I'd never commission
   my Pearlstein portraiture,
   afraid that my generous nature
   would be spread to the east and west,
   exposing my polar bearings
   to an unappreciative world
   or, worse, that my lean and hungry look
   would be preserved forever
   in a cross-legged, cross-eyed,
   cross-armed pose
   protective to a fault.

No, I want to be remembered
   --and I speak now in the ancient
   Pearlstinian tongue--
   as something between a fig leaf
   and a donut or as both sides
   in a game of tic-tac-toe.
   I mean the real me, with space bars
   and dos equis
   and openings and closings,
   hugs and kisses,
   the holey me and holy me
   all at once.

The naked truth, of course, is
   that the oyster is art
   whether open or closed
   and the stoney beauty of the pearl
   and the space that contains it
   exist either way;   27

but to one who must halve his oyster
and seed it too, the two only
dimensions hanging in some
hammock net from a picture molding
in a gallery seem not enough.

6

From the full-bodied, spaced-out
    flesh tones of Pearlstinian opulence,
    we descend
    to the fleshless space
    of Linhares' destitution
    where the span between the ribs
    is measured by the dry arroyos
    of the western plain;
    where the garden green vitality
    of a former lush valley
    has become the sickly pallor
    of mortal futility;
    where the man-sawed stumps
    rooted in the dry earth
    defy the force
    that severed them from life;
    and where the prognoses
    of cows and horses
    reach from the canvas
    toward my cold, happy heart,
    expiring and explaining themselves,
    and draw me into their
    blistering, tragic world.

Neither their bleating nor the natural
    moral example
    of Italian man twins
    suckled by a selfish wolf bitch
    can keep mankind
    from eating his steaks,
    from burning his logs,

from filling his pools,
for he has been suckled
by the same bitch
and nourishes only to use.

7

Lurching through the gallery
    seized first by one wall,
    then by another
    swinging high one moment,
    low the next,

We stumble into Vincent's world,
    our tongues continually dry
    as we realize
    that the ghastly green
    of our mortality
    relates us, rooted,
    to the cypress,
    that reaches, sways, extends,
    but at last remains.

Conscious of the wall--always the wall--
    our gallery is our field
    limited by a floor
    that refuses to go beyond
    and a redundant, celestial ceiling
    where even swirling stars
    cannot completely reach
    the fulfillment of each other,
    rooted as they are in space
    thrashing in their own seizures,
    yearning for release
    to merge, to mingle.

8

On the street from Brooklyn to Craft,
    from Frick to Gug,
    from Met to Moma to Whitney,
    the great centers mnemonically reduced
    to alphabetical rank
    because no other measure exists.

It is not so much the presence of art
    that enlivens the conversation,
    for when art exists
    it inspires silence,
    hushed tones, enforced
    from within or without
    (sometimes by some uniformed lover
    of art, some professional shusher hired
    to protect "The Forge" from its own
    deafening clang)
    a strange, tongue-tied, silent
    phenomenon of the body
    responding to the raptured soul.

No, the genuine conversation of art
    comes before, between, and beyond art
    in the enthusiasm
    of anticipation, transition, and memory.

It is thus the absence of art
    that inspires the chatter,
    the search for meaning,
    the lusty reaching,
    the correspondence,
    the intercourse of life.

It is eating thick pea soup
    on Madison Avenue
    in my London Fog sweater
    and his borrowing

three-quarters of an umbrella
from a corner stand
placed lovingly by some sunny soul
for some rainy day.

It is his disclaimer as instructor,
allowing his pupils to dilate
in their own directions
to beam their own lights
on their own canvases,
visualizing the universe
in the iridescence of their own
inner source
and confirming his pedagogic art.

It is the insistent, echoing beat
from twenty-one stories below
of the breakdance bass and trap,
enticing the mice
who escape from the theater <u>Cats</u>
across the street
and who stand in the snow
applauding eight acrobatic fleas
and dropping silver and copper.

It is the root of the squared Times
glimpsed just short
of the vanishing point
in a double-framed shadow box
of scrapers
reduced by twenty-first story
perspective from sky to street,
resisting the tendency to vanish
entirely in the rush to converge.

It is reading Whitman aloud in the snow
at Manahatta's shore,
realizing the reciprocal
life dependency of art and history
when a steel bridge

leaves the reverberating sounds
of "Crossing Brooklyn Ferry"
as the only remnant
of a transitory human experience.

It is Cro-Magnon woman
breathing the breath of 10,000 years
into the flute of the muse
continuing the spell,
making it happen
again in the anthro-apologetic
darkness
of homo sapien's cavernous heart.

It is the cadmium-white crust
of mastodon bones
extracted and thatched as roof
on the mud dwelling,
proof of the hunter's strength
when he ventured out,
of his vulnerability
when he huddled within.

It is eating Dominican black beans
and Bayamo's Chino-Latino cuisine
near the corner of Walk and Don't Walk
and the flaming people's car,
grotesque, armor plated
transplant from the Autobahn,
a comic comet rising
from the pit of Hell, its furor
again to threaten the night
with the acrid odor
of burning rope of hair.

It is the dyslexic Vesuvian transposition
of a "Fire from Naples"
and the mediterranean beach
at "Oceanside Park"
where we sat barefaced

with cuffs rolled up,
watching the lady in a fur coat
and waiting for the tide
to tickle our toes
and to emerse us all
in seeing water.

It is reading my verse aloud
to Yoruba Tribe Ibeji dolls,
surrogate twins asserting
their individuality,
disputing Warhol's quarter-hour
frame of a limitless horizon
while behind me watched
a whole wall of African masks
recording forever the event
in their silent oral history
without even one tsk-tsk
passing their open lips.

The conversation of art, of course,
is all that and more
and, given the failure
of my triptych to maintain
its composure,
I suppose I could digress
even further,
for any artist knows
the difficulty of crafting
a straight line and the
ease of recording a squiggle
and even the straight
must be fudged with illusion.

Our return to JFK was fudged:
We took the long way
across the Triboro Bridge
in order to get there faster.
And calling us back
were the sirens of the City,   33

screaming at our eyes and ears
beckoning back, promising
some mysterious fulfillment
in a giant, lofty banner waving
hello, goodbye and starting
my juices flowing all over again
as I jotted down the number
that seemed to offer an artist
decent odds: "(718) 786-fifty-fifty--
Loft for Rent."
Odds decent, that is, in a world
where all the questions
are framed in paint and motive
but where all the answers
are confined to dollars and cents.
And where the infinite spaces
between studio and gallery and museum
hardly fit within the same galaxy,
each stellar stop deserving
a universe of its own
in its silent, solitary
yearning to be.

The Messenger
Is Filled With Wrath

POST MORTEM

The woman yawns;
She looks around.
The yard is full of stones.
Weary she is of having to choose
A stone that's not her own.

STARING AT THE SPACE IN WORD JAM
LEFT BY GENE BLACK

Someone's always hitting
The Space Bar
Too soon.
There is no space
In WordJam
No space to think
No space to escape
No space to bridge.
Some damn fool
Somewhere
Left a space
That we're expected
To fill
Without a backspace key.
And who the hell
Stole the ribbon
From this thing!

DIVINING SNAKE RIVER

fixed motionless
at the base
of grave deep
canyons
the snake
remains suspended
like some collosal carrion
museum mounted
with twenty-two rattles
still attached
plus a button
of lost hopes
the scaled walls
carved from solid lava, flows
prophesy the futility
of conquest
in the face of cooling
passion
damming decision
or human scavenger's
fleeting heartbeat

COUPLETS ON THE DEATH OF AN IDEA

(A Discourse Between a Disenfranchised Voice and a Chorus of Its Peers)

(The Voice is loud throughout the reading. At first assertive, it becomes defensive, then vulnerable, then resigned.)

(The Chorus always speaks in a thoughtful whisper.)

V: I am not a trouble maker.
Ch: My topic sentences always control my paragraphs.

V: I am a vital, relevant part of my environment.
Ch: My paragraphs always support my topic sentences.

V: I have always supported the right cause.
Ch: My topic sentence is strong and assertive.

V: I have always gladly dropped any irrelevant idea, person, thing, quality in a confident unification of my existence.
Ch: My paragraph always adjusts to the reality expressed in my topic sentence.

40

V: I am satisfied with my lifestyle
     and I defy others to change it.
Ch: My topic sentence is never
     threatened by ideas that crop up
     unexpectedly in my writing.

V: I tend to speak rationally with
     regular eye contact and in a strong,
     assertive tone without pauses.
Ch: My teachers have always rewarded
     me for supporting my topic sentences.

V: I respect authority and willingly
     follow its lead.
Ch: My topic sentence governs my decisions
     in the world of my paragraph.

V: I recognize that some parts of my
     existence must be sacrificed if my
     life message is to be clearly
     expressed and understood.
Ch: My topic sentence always exerts its
     power to sweep away the ambiguous
     ideas in my paragraph.

V: I sometimes feel irrelevant in my
     own life's script.
Ch: My topic sentence is a ruthless
     dictator of its environment.

V: I sometimes sense that my family or
     friends would be able to function
     more easily if I did not exist.
Ch: My topic sentence always conveys a
     satisfying aura when the last
     irrelevancy is purged from my
     paragraph.

V: As a child, I was able to generate,
     to invent, new ideas from my environ-
     ment.   41

Ch: My topic sentences have helped
me learn to change my environment
to fit their needs.

V: On rare occasions, I remember
the freedom of my life before
I learned the value of obsessive
obedience.

Ch: As I fashion my college paragraph,
I yearn for the time when I will
be free to keep my best ideas.

V: As I close the garage door, I feel
satisfied that I am doing the only
thing I can do to preserve the
integrity of family and friends.

Ch: As I close my notebook, I know
that the sacrifice of any idea
is a small price for the peace
of mind that accompanies unity
in my paragraph.

ON RESISTING THE ATTEMPT
BY THE STATE OF TEXAS SYSTEM OF INJUSTICE
TO MAKE MY BIRTHDAY RELEVANT WITH THE DEATH
OF GARY GRAHAM, JUNE 3, 1993

I do not know Gary Graham

Of Death Row, Texas

But I share his anger,

Not in the same degree

But I do share his anger.

And not his present anger

But his original anger,

His first realization

That he was irrelevant

In this disunified

National Paragaph.

Not his anger at the Texas State

System of Injustice.

No, I share his anger

As a child

Entering a classroom

Bitter beyond his years already

At the age of ten

But willing to learn.

I share his anger

At a reading teacher

Who cast the matrix

Of his future,

A reading teacher

Whose disunified paragraphs
She insisted were whole,
Who set the doubts
Working in the faithful
Heart of a small boy.
I share his anger
At his discovery
Of the professional challenge
To his uncommon
Sense of idea decorum.
Shame!
Shame on the adult blindness
That calls disunity
Whole!
That models the texts
That lead only
To a child's confusion!
Ah! Confusion!
Would that we could view
Forever
The world through dazed double vision,
The drunken stupor
That relieves the pain
Of disillusion.
But a wise ten year old
Knows the nonsense

Of the adulteration
Of truth.
A wise child will rise
From confusion
To resentment
Of a system that fills
Its texts
With disunity
And winks at the plight
Of Gary Graham, child cynic.

I do not know Gary Graham
Of Death Row, Texas,
But I share his anger
At the writing teacher
Who failed his paragraph
For displaying the disunity
Of the reading text models.
And whose constant cry
To bolster up
Some topic sentence--
A child's first prison--
That must never be challenged
Even by the most
Compelling contradictory
Evidence
That must be trashed
In the systematic insanity   45

Of a curriculum
That demands unified
Paragraphs
Modeled on disunity.

I do not know Gary Graham
Of Death Row, Texas,
But I do share his anger
At a system of injustice
That dismisses him
And his story
Irrelevant to some
Concocted unified Texas Paragraph
Of Trial and Error.

And just to prove
My unbiased judgement,
I admit my understanding
Of the source of judicial
Blindness.
For they all shared
The same fourth grade teacher--
The judge, the jury,
The attorneys,
And poor Gary Graham
Of Death Row, Texas.
And they all learned
46

The same lesson
That irrelevancies are always
Dropped
From disunified paragraphs.
All except
Poor Gary Graham
Who got it in his head
Somehow--but not in school--
That the authority
Of a topic sentence
Is meant
In a democracy
To change
To fit existing evidence
And that sometimes an irrelevancy
Can assert itself
Until even the Topic Sentence
In the State House in Austin
Can adjust to the new Truth
And the irrelevancy becomes relevant
And the World
Is whole again.

LISTEN TO THE WORDS;
THEN SEND A CHILD TO OPEN THE DOOR

The messenger
Is filled
With wrath.
He would destroy
The infidel
As he sits
At Seder
Mouthing platitudes
Of generations
While playing
Pharoah's role
Exalted
On his left lean.
So send someone
With faith
Whose tongue
Trips on the trope.
Send one
Who wits not to ask
Whose gentle innocence
Can stare
The messenger down
Whose sense of exclusion
Includes us all.

Celebrating Space

THE UNDERSTANDING

Finding a level place to stand
Is first priority
Living on the side of a hill
In Globe, Arizona;
That and
Keeping it once you've found it.
Ten-foot retaining walls
Make yards of canyons
And give the illusion
Of foothold
For a couple of generations
Until the mortar matures and dissolves
And the wall stones
Drop ten feet
To scatter on the yard below.

A real oldtimer
Can remember
Where each stone belongs
And can place it again
With new, stronger mortar
Within the weakening wall
In hopes that the collapse
Can be avoided.
For finding a level place to stand 53

Is first priority
Living on the side of a hill
In Globe, Arizona.

At the age of ten,
I could not have known
The relative importance
Of my garden play yard.
It was all of creation
That I knew
And what existed
Above or below
Did not intrude.
That it might slip someday
Or be boulder littered
From above
Seemed beyond my youthful need
To know.
My sheltered shade
Of pomegranate columns
Kept the sand cool
And soft
And my hundred lead soldiers
Could offer up the sacrifice,
Could pretend a war,
54

And retire friends
To their drawer.

At the age of ten,
I could not have known
That every level place to stand
Is formed
By packing sod against the wall,
By filling the canyon
With the old, the broken,
The once essential artifacts,
Until the yard emerges flat.
At the age of ten,
I could not have known
The cast iron outcrop
From my soft soldier sand
Would cause a truce
To dig in depths
Never tried,
To discover in the rusted
Sand encrusted frame
The remnants
Of a Singer treadle
And eventually the whole useful
Useless tangle   55

That given meaning
Forty years hence
Would form an understanding.

SEARCHING FOR BIRTHDAY ON PAGE 150
OF MY DICTIONARY OF THE AMERICAN LANGUAGE

It is not an easy birth
That proceeds
From an Autonomous Region,
In the Russian
Ethniscape Birobijan,
Certified, Designated, Mehitza-Protected
Bima, inaccessible
Evidence of Socialist
Just Revenge,
The non-Pogrom
That cannot justify
The weight of all the others:
Birobijan, the Jewish Autonomous Region.
From there emanates
The impetuous birr,
The emphatic statement
That announces the paradoxic gush
Ending bearing,
Beginning birth.
Any control of birth
Loses its meaning

After the fact.
It is the day that marks the birth
Or the mark that dates it.
Only the place is certain.
As a firstborn,
As a b'hor,
I was accompanied
With no issues
Of birthrate or right.
Such concerns were the product
Eighteen months hence
Of my brother's arrival.
But such issues
Of the world I enter
Say less of who I am
Than the painful certifications
Of the Birobijani world
I leave,
A leaving without tonic
Beneficial Birthwort
For the brutal
Stamped approval
To be.
58

IN MEMORY OF A SNOWFLAKE

Little snowflake, where're you going,
Flying to and fro?
Don't you have a set direction?
Don't you have a place to go?

Scurrying by in winter's whiteness,
Flurrying high with every gust,
We can see your fluffy lightness
As you scamper close to us.

What makes you, snowflake, so like people,
Running back and forth so fast,
Skipping 'round in tiny circles
Always busy, dizzy, tizzy,
Busy, busy till the last?

So like people, little snowflake,
When you finally come to rest,
You melt right into your surroundings,
Vow to stay; this place is best!

So like people, little snowflake,
Promised never more to fly,
Still, it isn't many minutes
Till your new-found home is dry.

So like people, little snowflake!
I thought your plans were made to stay.
I wonder where you've gone and flown to
And if for good you've gone away.

So like people, little snowflake!
Gone so quickly from this place.
Never more to see a snowing.
What's that? Why, hello, snowflake!
Where're you going?

BLOWING UP ON A PARKING LOT
OF A NUCLEAR POWER PLANT
(MEMENTO FOR JEREMY)

"The trick is in the thumb--"
He had engaged a nuclear physicist
In continuous conversation,
Discussing atoms and neutrons
Ad infinitessimal.
But now it was my turn.
"The trick," I said, "is in the thumb.
Pull the opening around the thumb
And under."
He had spent the tour
Through Rancho Seco Nuclear
Generating Plant
In his own curious search,
Speaking computer jargon
From his eleven-year perspective
With the best--
Of Fortran, Cobal, Language Fourth,
But on the way to the car
In the middle of the parking lot,
He gave his Grandpa a chance to perform.
No physicists were in sight

So it was my privilege
To answer his request
To teach him
How to tie the end
Of his blue, souvenir balloon,
A subject, I guess, that had been saved
By his school
For his sixth year.
My contribution to his advanced status
Would be his ability
To give his balloon form
With his own breath
And then to give that form
A moment of permanence.

SOMETIMES I WISH MY NAME WERE GONZALEZ

Sometimes I wish
My name were Gonzalez.
But then, I know,
They would call me Ramirez
Or Lopez
Or Santiago.
As it is they call me Cohen
Or Kaplan
Or Greenberg.
I guess I should be satisfied
That finally I am approaching
My destination
Albeit in some mysterious,
Circuitous way,
A destination that I have
At once
Attempted to avoid
And yearned to achieve.
For to become a mensch--a person,
An individual, a dignified self--
I sometimes have darted away
Alone
Hoping to earn my place

In my community by leaving
Them behind.

But others will not allow
Me to forget.
For when they stammer
My name,
They place me where I belong.
They remind me
That my centuries old
Soul
Finds its calling
In the breath
Of thousands of blessings
That have brought me
To this place.

How is it, then,
Understanding my own
Ambiguity so well,
That I stammer your name?
How is it that I somehow
Return your soul
To its origin
For some validation
Of its own individuality?

Why is it such effort
To differentiate Alicia
From Margarita in my classroom
And why do their names substitute
So easily, so glibly on my tongue
For each other?
And should we be insulted
When we are thus returned
Without reward
To our first sense of self?
Or is it in truth
Only an inarticulate honor
Of the clan
To which we belong
And to which we owe
Some homage?

When I catch your eye
On the mall
On some Thursday evening
And when you catch mine,
What uncertainty
Causes me to turn away
To avoid stammering
Your name?

And when we meet
In some silent mall
On some higher plane
Where names and clans
Have lost their use,
Will our souls embrace
Without excuse?

ENDING DROUGHT WITH AN ACT OF KINDNESS: THE EARTH'S ANSWER TO KINDNESS IN SOMALIA

I am Earth Mother!
I am your home!
I charge you!
Tell these words to your children
When you lie down
When you rise up
And when you walk by the way.

If you fail,
I will withhold
The former rain
And the latter rain
And you shall perish.

If you hear my children cry
And you do not feed them,
I will parch your lakes
And silence your rivers.
If you hear my children cry
And do not heal them,
I will scatter your clouds
And vanish the glisten
Of your grassy dew.

If you hear my children cry
And you do not nourish
Their spirits,
I will grind your fields
To dust
And wither the crops
That would fill your belly.

But if you tell these words
To your children
When you lie down
When you rise up
And when you walk by the way,
I will send you
The former rain
And the latter rain
And you shall prosper.

If you share even one sweet morsel
With my children,
I will flood your Honey Lake.
If you touch the stretched skin
Of the haggard face
Of my children in love,
I will fill your Calaveras Reservoir.

If you cause one smile
To grace the face of my children,
I will return sparkle to the surface
Of Clear Lake.
If you add beauty to the life
Of even one child for one moment,
I will raise Buena Vista Lake to its brim.
If you place one stone upon another
To begin a shelter for one child,
I will replenish Stone Canyon Reservoir.
If you bless my children
With a rebirth of hope,
I will fill Nacimiento Reservoir.
If you affirm the ancient traditions
Of my families, my tribes,
I will remember Mono Lake and Cachuma
Reservoir and Havasu Lake.
If you supply my children
With protection and motivation,
I will fortify the waters
Of Lake Arrowhead and Vaquero Reservoir.
If you touch the soul
Of my children,
I will overflow the banks
Of Lake Almanor.

If you cause the spirit
Of my children to soar,
I will cause the reflection
Of the blue sky
To be seen again in Eagle Lake.

Tell these words to your children
When you lie down
When you rise up
And when you walk by the way.
And I, your Earth Mother,
Will send you
The former rain
And the latter rain
And you shall prosper.

THE ANSWER IS SUSPENDED IN THE SKY

The answer is suspended
In the sky.
Wilt thou take--
Or not?
Will some cloud
Obscure the promise,
Delay the answer,
Extend the sixth day
Beyond its limits
Or will one star
Signal the initial sibilant
In the ageless renewal?
"Shh!"
Twilight
Rustles the trees
As day's heat
Gives way to hints of evening cool.

Wilt thou take,
Oh Israel,
Or not?
Will some distraction
Divert the answer

To some adjacent
Galaxy
Or will a second point of light
Raise expectations,
Renew commitment
In the child's pointing finger:
"Aba!"
Father exists there
As here.

Wilt thou,
Oh Israel,
Take this Bride?
"Shh! Aba!"
"Shh! Aba!"
In the final, glimmering
Recognition,
The answer is revealed.
Gently tinted horizon
Suspends the fragile
Three-star chain
In the new darkness
As Father
Responds
With the final "Tov!"

"Shh! Aba! Tov!"
"Shh! Aba! Tov!"
"Shh! Aba! Tov!"

"Shabbat Tov!"
"Shabbat Tov."

SHABBAT SPACE:
DREAMING   ON THE CUSP

I celebrate space.
I celebrate weddings.
I celebrate ladders.
And Michaelangelo
And Chagall
And Jacob.
I defy gravity
And surface tension
And proclaim
Independence
And dependency.
I celebrate neither here nor there,
But the space that defines
Both here and there.
For I am a Gemini,
And I am of the undecided,
The indefinite.
I dream on the cusp,
And I am lifted by the wind,
Plummeting in my stoop to pray

Or to scavenge,
Descending three stories
In a single bound
Explosive volume
Of art filling lofts
And galleries
And museums
And historical fiction
And fictitious history.
I neither walk
Nor run,
But skip
And skim,
One foot always reaching
Limited not by time
Nor space
But enabled by them.
Finding meaning
Only in them
And in nothing else.
Vaulting six days
Giving past and future holy meaning
In a momentary rest,
Lifting my Spirit
Again
To soar

And to plunge
And to celebrate
This breath
This life
This holy space.

Explanations

EXPLANATIONS

p. 57   "Searching for Birthday"

Birobijan--In the Soviet Union,
a designated place for the
encouragement of Jewish culture.

Mehitza-Protected--the curtain
that separates men from women in
a traditional synagogue. In this
poem, the curtain that separates
the city of Birobijan from the
rest of the world.

Bima--the raised platform in a
synagogue where the public reading
of the Torah takes place.

non-pogrom--Birobijan must be seen
in stark contrast with the pervasive
anti-semitism throughout Europe.
A pogrom is the attack upon a
Jewish shtetl or ghetto to plunder,
kill, or strike fear in to Jewish
hearts.

b'hor--a firstborn Jewish son who
holds special observance of Passover
in remembrance of G-d's sparing
the firstborn sons of Jews in
Egypt prior to the Exodus.

p. 67   "Ending Drought with an Act of
        Kindness"--Within a few days of

our sending aid to Somalian victims
of starvation, California's drought
of several years ended. We often
forget acts of human kindness, but
the Earth remembers.

p. 71   "The Answer is Suspended in the
Sky"--Jewish tradition says that
the Sabbath (Shabbat) begins
when three stars appear in the
evening sky.

this Bride--Jews see the Sabbath
as their beautiful bride.

Aba--Father

Tov--Good

Shabbat Tov--Good Sabbath